Chinese New Year!

CHELSEA KONG

© 2024-2025 Chelsea Kong

All rights reserved. All images used in this book are licensed copies from their respectful owners including Freepik, Ghetty Images, Canva, others. This book or any portion thereof may not be reproduced or used in any manner whatsoever without the express written permission of the publisher except for the use of brief quotations in a book review.

Printed in 2024-2025, Made in Toronto, Canada
ISBN: 978-1-998335-14-5
Library and Archives Canada

Chinese New Year is often from January 20 to February 21 on the Western calendar. It's the start of the Chinese calendar year. They wear traditional clothing, usually red.

The Chinese calendar is the lunar year.
There is an extra month and no leap year.
People in China get 7 days off work.
In China, it's very important.

China also calls it the Spring Festival.
Families will begin the festival on the Eve.
This is celebrated for 15 days.
After this, they have the Lantern festival.

Chinese say, "Wish you enlarge your wealth"
Gong xi fa cai / Gong hei fat choi:
simplified Chinese: 恭喜发财;
traditional Chinese: 恭喜發財;

After the Gong xi fa cai / Gong hei fat choi, people greet and shake hands.
Bless each other to have a prosperous year.
Blessed health, joy, peace, unity, jobs, increase, favour, more than enough, and more.

Beautiful paper lanterns are lit up.
It is a time for celebration.
Everyone helps to prepare to celebrate.

Parents and grandparents give money,
Money is put in a red envelope.
We call it a red pocket.

This is money used in China.
There are different coloured dollar bills.
Money is put in a purse, pouch, and bag.

Parents keep the money safe.
It is not opened until the next day.
Chinese think they will have good luck.

A married man and woman get gold jewelry, lots of money and gifts on the wedding day. Red pocket money is for unmarried people.

The red paper that is hung on the door frame to keep bad spirits out.
This is like the Jews using blood on the door frames of their house at Passover.

Beautiful paper lanterns hang from above.
They light the way in the night.
Be careful of the light inside.

Firecrackers are used to celebrate.
There are different firecrackers.
Parents should be there to help.

China town and China are crowded. People walk, take the public transportation, and others pay for other rides.

It is busy this time of year.
People are outside, and there is a lot to do.
There are people even in the park.

Restaurants and buffets are busy too.
Special prices are used for the new year.
Grocery stores also have sales.

People will travel to China to celebrate.
Some will stay for a whole month.
Hotels are busy.
Flights can be expensive.

Stores are busy for the Chinese New Year.
More street vendors are found.
They make the most money at the festivals.

Chinese eat dumplings, rice, and noodles,
Noodles means a long life.
Families can be make them at home.

Children can learn and make dumplings.
Dumplings look like coin purses.
This means wealth and prosperity.

Fruit salad is fun and easy to make.
Children love to make the fruit salad.
Parents will make dinner and dessert.

Lobster   Crab   Shrimp

Lobster: good marriage and prosperity.
Crab: excellent career.
Shrimp: liveliness.

Chicken   Rice (Heaven and Earth)

Chicken means joy, completion, prosperity, and togetherness of the family.
Rice is fertility, wealth, and luck.

Abalone   Peking duck

Abalone: good fortune.
Peking duck: fertility.
These foods are expensive.

Mushrooms   Broccoli

Mushrooms is long life and opportunities.
Broccoli can mean a close family tie.
Mixed vegetables means family harmony.

Fish

Fish is steamed and it means abundance.
Cooked with green onion, and ginger.
Hot oil and soya sauce is poured on top.

Egg | Spring rolls

Egg dyed red: fertility and prosperity.
Spring rolls: gold, wealth, prosperity
and it is crispy.

Bamboo   Tangerine

Bamboo shoots are long life,
wealth, and wishes.
Tangerine is happiness and good luck.

Almond cookies   **Fa Gao - Prosperity cake**

Almond cookies means financial happiness
and they are wealth.
Fa Gao means wealth and prosperity.

Black moss
"fat choy"

Chinese New Year
Restaurant dish

Black moss that looks like hair is
grown in the desert.
This is wealth or good fortune.
The Chinese New Year dish must be eaten.

Tray of togetherness is given to others.
The Chinese say it is luck and fortune.
There are different snacks and candy.

After dinner, people have a dessert.
Chinese love to make lots and share.
Family and relatives celebrate together.

Tang yuan

Sesame balls

Each family has a different dessert. Tang yuan is a dough ball with sweet paste. Tang yuan is unity, both with your loving partner, and with your family.

 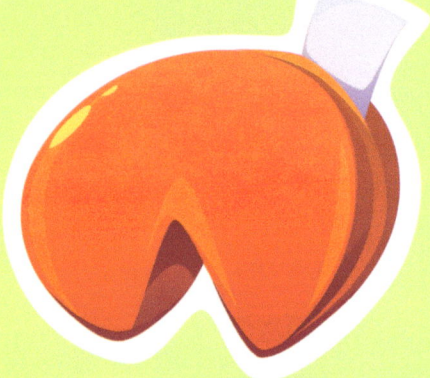

steamed peach shaped bun with sweet paste inside   **fortune cookie**

A peach shaped bun is a long life.
Fortune cookies are growth or alive.
Wishes are shared and are important.
Jesus blesses us with the best.

People believe the lotus flower means purity.
They have a spiritual touch.
Christians are made pure and spiritual
through their faith through Jesus Christ.

Chinese also sing Gong Xi Fa Cai.
Some people do the lion dance to celebrate.
Some people play the drums.
A lion follows comes and a man with a fan.

Lion dance means power, to be superior, wisdom, and brings prosperity. Christians believe in Jesus Christ. He is the Lion of Judah.

The dragon plays with a ball on a stick.
Many Chinese believe the dragon dance
means wisdom, power, and wealth,
and brings good luck.

Satan makes himself the dragon.
Jesus Christ wins against Satan.
He has given the authority, power, rule,
long life that never ends, and all blessings
to His people.

China has fireworks to celebrate.
Chinese have a big celebration.
It is a beautiful night.

Chinese New Year blessing.
Speak words that will encourage and bless
Speak with love, faith, joy, and hope.

Those who are married need blessings.
This keeps the peace, joy, love, and unity.
God's Word has all the blessings you need.

Christians will pray to bless their food.
Prayer makes it clean and healthy to eat.
We plead the blood of Jesus over it.

Get blessings from parents and adults. God's blessings last for a thousand generations and keep growing everyday.

MY CHINESE TRADITIONAL CLOTIHING COLLECTION

Here are my vests and jackets.
Chinese also wear dresses.
You can find clothes for men and children.
The Chinese malls sometimes have sales.

References

Lindsary Parrill, "Chinese New Year: 10 Traditional Foods and What They Symbolize"
Digital Trends Group and The Manual, 2024.
https://www.themanual.com/food-and-drink/chinese-new-year-food-meanings/

Nations Online. "Food Symbolism During Chinese New Year Celebrations" Nations Online, 2024.
https://www.nationsonline.org/oneworld/chinese_customs/food_symbolism.htm

References

Lesley Kennedy,"10 Symbolic Foods of Lunar New Year"
A&E Television Networks, LLC, 2024.
https://www.history.com/news/symbolic-foods-of-chinese-new-year

Wariya Intreyonk. "Chinese New Year Food and Their Meanings" Gastronomer Lifestyle (Thailand) Company Limited, 2024.
https://gastronomerlifestyle.com/chinese-new-year-food-and-their-meanings/

SALVATION PRAYER

God, I know I sinned against you. Forgive me for the wrong that I have done. I believe that Jesus Christ died on the cross for me. That He rose from the grave so that after three days. I can have His long-lasting life. Come into my heart to be my Lord and Savior. I choose to turn away from my sins and I choose to follow you. Lead me to walk with you. Keep me safe and teach me your ways. Stop every bad thing in my life that has an open door to hurt me. Close those doors. Holy Spirit, fill me now in Jesus' name. Amen.

BAPTISM IN THE HOLY SPIRIT

Jesus, you are the one that fills me with Your Spirit. Come Holy Spirit and come into my life and fill me to overflow with Your presence. Come with your fire too. Thank you for the gift of tongues in Jesus' name. Amen.

Open your mouth and let the words come out that God gives you. It will be words that you don't know what they mean. You can ask God what it means. You need to let Him talk through you every day to grow this gift.

He will bring you closer to God and you will know Jesus more. You will have power from God to do great things and know things.

PRAYER

Thank you, Father God, for this book on Chinese New Year. Thank you for teaching me about the culture, food, and more. Thank you for safety against Satan and for winning against him. Thank you for keeping my family and friends safe, too. Teach me to bless others and to see it your way. Thank you for blessings, health, success, joy, peace, and unity. Bless my family and friends to have these too. Thank you for everything bless you have for us in Jesus' name. Amen.

Message from the Author

Thank you for reading this book. I hope you can leave a good review to encourage me to write more books to teach children and adults. The Lord blesses you with all that you do. May you experience all his blessings in your life and for your family too. Please share this book with others. The Lord will bless you more. There may be content about the Chinese New Year that is not in this book, but I chose what most people need to know and the most important foods. I wrote with a Christian view. Most of the culture and practice are not Christian. I wanted to create a faith-based celebration. In 2025, Chinese New Year is March 1-15.

OTHER PRODUCTS

- Knowing God
- How to Hear God's Voice
- New Life in Jesus
- Loving Israel
- God's Gifts/Spiritual Talents
- Meeting God
- Word Power
- Fruit of the Spirit
- The Tabernacle
- Bride for Jesus
- A Life of Prayer
- Live Free
- Who am I in Jesus
- Walk in Love
- God's Favor
- Man of God
- Woman of God
- How to Use Money
- God's Wisdom
- Fasting
- See Jerusalem and Bethany
- First Fruit Offering
- Feast of Trumpets
- Day of Atonement
- Feast of Tabernacles
- Counting the Omer
- Festival of Lights
- Glory, Presence, and Holy Spirit
- Live in God's Presence
- Pentecost
- See Galilee, Nazareth, and Tiberias
- Hear God Speak
- Knowing Jesus
- Knowing Holy Spirit
- A Healthy Life and Healthy Life Work Book
- Smokey the Cat
- Passover Unleavened Bread
- Resurrection Life
- The Blessing
- Revival
- Chelsea Learns Hebrew
- Thanksgiving
- Give Thanks
- Jesus Birth
- Loving Jesus: Bride and Groom
- Proverbs 31 Woman

OTHER PRODUCTS

ABC of People in the Bible
Colours in the Bible
Breakthroughs
Open Doors
The Seven Spirits of God
Numbers in the Bible
Aglee the Eagle
An Eagle's Life
Chelsea Learns Numbers in Hebrew
ABC's of Faith
Feast of Purim
A Royal Life
Family Day
Family Blessings

Coming soon
Worship
Pandas
Canada
Animal Stories
Eagles
Fun in Caribbean

Devotionals
31 Day Devotional

Inspirational/Other
Chelsea's Psalms and Poems
Your Daily Meal: Chelsea's Photo Album

Puzzle Books
Biblical Puzzle Book Vol 1-5
Bible Puzzles for Young Children Book 1-3
Biblical Puzzle for Children Books 1-5

Coming soon
Chelsea's Psalms and Poems 2
Travel West Caribbean
Chelsea's Bible Puzzles

OTHER PRODUCTS

Teaching Series

How to Hear God's Voice Teaching Guide & Audio Book

Relationship with God, Jesus, Holy Spirit Guide

Knowing God, Jesus, Holy Spirit Guide & Audio Book

Flowing in the Prophetic

Teaching (Non-Sale on my website)

Purim

Passover

Resurrection

BOOK REVIEWS

More books on Amazon, Kobo, and Barnes and Noble, Smashwords, and IngramSpark.
https://chelseak532002550.wordpress.com/

More books on Amazon, Kobo, and Barnes and Noble, Smashwords, and IngramSpark.
https://www.amazon.com/author/chelseakong

Please leave a review and share with friends to help the author continue to write more books to reach more readers. Thank you so much for your support.

Review!

About
CHELSEA KONG

She is a writer, creative arts and digital media artist, skilled administration and certified PCP (Payroll Compliance Professional), and podcaster. Chelsea also served in a variety of roles, from audiovisual, photography, to assisting on the worship team, and ministry team. She also has a passion for families being united.

Chelsea has been a guest on Unity Live Radio, The Lady Tracey Show, and How to Live for Christ and is highly recommended by a Proud Christian blog. She is also a guest blogger. A few of her books have been featured in YourAuthorHub, etc. She graduated from Hotel and Restaurant Management, Digital Media Arts, Office Administration, Payroll Compliance Professional, and experience working with children. Chelsea lives in Toronto, Canada. She mainly writes children's books, stories, bridal writing, poems, lyrics for songs, words of encouragement, blessings, prayers, and jokes. The author of How to Hear the Voice of God, the Bridal Collection, Knowing God, etc. She also has her own Bible Puzzle books and other inspired products. Her podcast channel is called Chelsea K on Anchor, Spotify, and iTunes.

Please check my website to find out more:
https://chelseak532002550.wordpress.com/

www.ingramcontent.com/pod-product-compliance
Lightning Source LLC
Chambersburg PA
CBHW042006150426
43194CB00003B/146